I'M A FUTURE FOOD SCIENTIST!

Written By
Manisha Nayak

Illustrated By
Eliz Ong

WS Education
NEW JERSEY • LONDON • SINGAPORE • BEIJING • SHANGHAI • TAIPEI • CHENNAI

Published by
WS Education Pte. Ltd.
5 Toh Tuck Link, Singapore 596224

National Library Board, Singapore Cataloguing in Publication Data
Name(s): Nayak, Manisha. | Ong, Eliz, illustrator.
Title: I'm a future food scientist! / written by Manisha Nayak ; illustrated by Eliz Ong.
Other Title(s): I'm a future scientist!
Description: Singapore : WS Education, [2026]
Identifier(s): ISBN 978-981-98-1034-5 (hardcover) | 978-981-98-1035-2 (paperback) | 978-981-98-1036-9 (book for institutions) | 978-981-98-1037-6 (book for individuals)
Subject(s): LCSH: Food--Research--Juvenile literature. | Food engineers--Juvenile literature. | Food--Research--Juvenile literature.
Classification: DDC 664--dc23

British Library Cataloguing-in-Publication Data
A catalogue record for this book is available from the British Library.

Desk Editor: Daniele Lee

Printed in Singapore

CONTENTS

Say 'Hello' to Avo!

What's your favourite food? There are so many different types of food around us that it can get hard to choose just one. Did you know that there is loads of science behind how food is grown, what is in our food and why it tastes so good?

Food scientists are people who study the nature and quality of food. From analysing the flavour, texture and nutritional value of food, to carrying out food safety tests, to researching and creating new food items, there is never a dull moment in the life of a food scientist!

Read on and get to know all about the exciting world of food science!

All the best!

The Science of Food

Food science is a fascinating field of study. Let's look at some ways in which food science can be beneficial for us!

Better and more food

As the population of the world increases, we need more and more food. Food science helps us to grow more food efficiently. Advancements in food science and technology have allowed farmers to improve the quality and quantity of their crops. Food science can also help us to make food production more sustainable.

Many food scientists work in greenhouses to find ways to grow food of a better quality.

More nutritious food

Food science helps to improve the nutritional quality of food. Food can be enhanced to meet specific dietary needs. For example, some types of bread and cereal are fortified with iron, which can help prevent iron deficiency in people.

Biscuits fortified with vitamins and iron

WORD WHIZ

fortified: made stronger
deficiency: a lack or shortage

Something for everyone

Food science has helped many people enjoy food that they are usually not able to consume. For example, some people are unable to eat dairy products as their bodies are not able to digest lactose, which is a substance found in milk. Food science has made it possible to produce lactose-free milk and yoghurt.

Lactose-free milk

Many people cannot digest a substance called gluten, which is found in bread and cakes. Thanks to food scientists, gluten-free options are now available.

Gluten-free bread

Let's preserve it!

Food science helps to ensure that food does not spoil easily and remains safe for consumption. Food science has made it possible for food to be preserved for longer periods, using methods such as freezing and canning.

Freezing fruits and vegetables can help to preserve them for a longer time.

Canned food does not spoil as quickly as fresh food.

Behind the Bite

Have you ever taken a close look at the food you eat? Different parts of our food come from different sources. Some come from plants, while others come from animals. Let's take a closer look!

Milk comes from animals, such as cows and goats. Some types of milk also come from plants, such as soybean or almond plants.

Eggs come from animals, such as chickens and ducks.

Know Your Nutrients!

The food we eat gives us energy to work and play. However, did you know that energy is not the only thing that we get from food?

Food contains many substances that are essential to keep us healthy. These substances are known as nutrients. The essential nutrients that we get from food are carbohydrates, proteins, fats, vitamins, minerals and water.

Nutrients that our bodies need in larger amounts are called macronutrients. These include water, proteins, carbohydrates and fats.

Nutrients that our bodies need in small amounts are known as micronutrients. Examples include vitamins and minerals.

Carbohydrates

Carbohydrates are our main source of energy. Carbohydrates can be found in rice, wheat, pasta, potatoes, fruits and milk.

Fibre is a type of carbohydrate that does not provide us with energy, but it has many important functions in the body. It absorbs water and helps keep our digestive system healthy. Fibre is found in fruits and vegetables.

Fats

Fats are sources of energy that can be stored in our bodies. The body uses fats to maintain its temperature and protect important organs. Cooking oils, nuts, fish and avocados are healthy sources of fats.

Some fats, like those found in processed foods, can be harmful. Taking them in large amounts can lead to heart disease.

Proteins

Proteins are nutrients that help our bodies to grow and repair themselves. Proteins can be found in food such as meat, fish, eggs, beans and nuts.

Vitamins and minerals

Vitamins and minerals are essential to keep our bodies healthy. Vitamin A helps to keep our eyes healthy. The mineral calcium builds bones and teeth. Vitamins and minerals can be found in fruits, vegetables, whole grains, lean meats and dairy products.

Why do we drink water?

Water is also very important to keep your body healthy. Don't forget to drink enough water!

Mix and Match

Many food items you eat are actually different plant parts. Can you match the food items to the correct plant parts?

Food item	Plant part
Potato 	Leaf
Spinach 	Seed
Tomato 	Fruit
Pea 	Root
Carrot 	Stem

Find the answers on page 55!

The Little Farmers

Have you ever wondered why bees and butterflies are often seen around flowers? Well, they get food in the form of nectar from the flowers. In return, the flowers also benefit from the visiting insects. And, so do humans! Let's find out how!

Animals such as bees and butterflies play a significant part in the production of food for humans. When they visit flowers for food, they transfer pollen from one flower to another. The transfer of pollen from the male part of a flower to the female part is known as pollination.

WORD WHIZ

pollen: a yellow powdery substance found in the male parts of flowers

Pollination leads to the reproductive cells of the plant fusing. This process is called fertilisation. After fertilisation, flowers develop into fruits. The fruits contain seeds that can grow into new plants. In this way, animals help the plant to reproduce.

After pollination and fertilisation, the tomato flowers develop into fruits.

The fruits turn red as they ripen.

Humans also benefit greatly from this process as many of the fruits and seeds produced are sources of food for us!

Here are some more examples of food produced for us, thanks to the little farmers such as bees and butterflies!

Eggplant

Grapes

Bell peppers

Cucumbers

Find out which other animals help in pollination!

A Cool Solution

Do we need to keep the ice cream cake in the freezer so it doesn't melt?
There's no need to do that. The cake box has dry ice.
'Dry' ice?? What is dry ice?
Dry ice is solid carbon dioxide.

Carbon dioxide?? The gas?
Yes, carbon dioxide is a gas at room temperature, but it can be frozen and compressed into a solid.
Solid carbon dioxide, or dry ice, has special properties that make it very useful.
HAPPY BIRTHD

For example, dry ice is very handy when it comes to transporting frozen food.
HAPPY BIRTHD
It prevents food such as ice cream and ice cream cakes from melting too quickly.
DRY ICE
DRY ICE
!!
Oh, that's good. I wouldn't want our lovely ice cream cake to be a melted puddle!

Hmm... can't we just use regular ice to keep the ice cream cake frozen?
Good question. Let me give you some cold, hard facts.
Regular ice is not as cold as dry ice. It won't be able to keep the cake frozen.
Ice will also melt very quickly. The melted ice will create a messy puddle around the cake.

Ice
Dry ice
Dry ice is much, much colder than regular ice. It can keep frozen things frozen for a long time.
Also, unlike regular ice, dry ice does not melt into a liquid. It changes directly into a gas.
Oh! Is that why it's called 'dry' ice? Because it doesn't melt into water like regular ice?
You're right, Oscar! That's why you'll never see a puddle of melted dry ice.

How cold is dry ice?
About −78.5 °C!
Whoa! That's wayyyy colder than even our freezer, which has a temperature of −18 °C!
−18°C

Ooh, is this white smoke dry ice in its gaseous form?
No, that's not carbon dioxide. Carbon dioxide is invisible.
The air around the dry ice loses heat to the dry ice and becomes cold. Water vapour in the surroundings comes in contact with this cold air, loses heat and condenses into tiny water droplets, creating the white 'smoke' around the dry ice.

Oh! We learnt about condensation in school. That's how clouds are formed!
Yes! And so is the 'smoke' around the mouth of a kettle of boiling water!
The 'fog' effect of dry ice is also used in stage performances and movies!

Why does it say 'handle with care'?
DRY ICE HANDLE WITH CARE
Dry ice is so cold that touching it with your bare hands can cause frostbite! Be careful not to touch it!
Thank you for telling us so many 'cool' facts about dry ice, Mum and Dad!
The end

Is That Safe to Eat?

Have you ever felt sick after eating something? It could have been a case of food poisoning. Let's find out more!

Food poisoning occurs when we take in food or water contaminated with harmful germs, toxins or chemicals. In most cases, the food is contaminated by bacteria or viruses.

E. coli is a type of bacteria that can cause severe food poisoning.

WORD WHIZ

contaminated: made unclean or impure

The symptoms of food poisoning include nausea, vomiting, diarrhoea, stomach cramps and fever. You should see a doctor if you get food poisoning.

There are many reasons why food can get contaminated. Some food items contain bacteria that are usually killed during the cooking process. Eating these food items raw can cause the bacteria to enter your body and cause food poisoning.

Raw eggs may contain bacteria called salmonella that can cause food poisoning.

If food is not cooked properly, or prepared under unhygienic conditions, it may contain harmful germs. Food that is not stored properly or left out for too long can also cause food poisoning.

Uncovered food can attract germ-carrying houseflies, which can lead to food poisoning.

If hands have not been washed properly before preparing food, or if the person preparing the food is sick, food can get contaminated with germs.

Learn how to wash your hands effectively!

We must wash our hands thoroughly with soap and water before eating or preparing food.

Did You

The world is full of fascinating types of food. It is also full of fascinating food facts. Let's check out a few of them!

A cucumber is about 95% water!

The first pizza delivery to space happened in 2001. A six-inch salami pizza was delivered to the International Space Station (ISS), located about 400 kilometres above the Earth's surface.

How does a pizza party in space look?

Know?

A dye called carmine is used to give some food items their vibrant red or pink colour. Carmine is made from crushed cochineal insects!

Mushrooms are a type of fungus!

A grape sinks in water, but a watermelon floats! This is due to the fact that things that are less dense than water float on it. A grape is denser than water, but the air pockets in a watermelon make it less dense than water, causing it to float.

Cotton candy is 99% air!

I'm Inspired

Have you seen the word 'pasteurised' on some milk or juice cartons? The word comes from the name of Louis Pasteur, widely regarded as the world's first food scientist. Let's find out more!

Born in 1822, French microbiologist Louis Pasteur made significant contributions to the fields of vaccination, fermentation in food and food preservation.

Pasteur discovered that microorganisms are responsible for spoiling food and causing diseases.

Microorganisms can spoil milk and make it unfit for consumption.

Pasteur developed a process in which a food item or beverage is heated to a specific temperature for a set period of time. This helps to kill the harmful microorganisms that cause illness, and preserve the food for a longer time. This process is called pasteurisation and it is widely used to preserve milk, juices and other products.

Normally, fresh milk would go bad in just a few hours. Consuming it could make us sick. Thanks to pasteurisation and refrigeration, we can enjoy the freshness of milk for several days!

The Tiny Chefs

We often associate microorganisms such as bacteria and fungi with food spoilage. However, did you know that some of them actually play a significant role in making some types of food?

Bacteria

Some types of bacteria are used to turn milk into different foods such as yoghurt and cheese.

Yeast

Yeast is a type of fungus that is used to make food such as bread. It causes the bread dough to rise and gives bread its airy texture.

Detective Work

Take a close look at these pictures of food items from around the world. Can you identify them correctly?

Find the answers on page 55!

A 'Hot' Topic

What was the spiciest food you ever ate? Did your tongue feel like it was on fire? Did your eyes water? Did you break out in a sweat? These are some reactions that some people have when they eat very spicy food, like chilli peppers!

Words such as 'hot' or 'burning' are often used to describe spicy food, even though the food may not actually have a high temperature. So where does the sensation of heat come from?

The heat we feel when we bite into a chilli pepper is not actually a taste. The burning feeling comes from our body's pain response system.

Chilli peppers contain a substance called capsaicin, which activates receptors found inside our mouth and on our tongue. The function of these receptors is to detect heat. When they are activated, they send a signal to the brain. The brain is tricked into thinking that the food is hot and is burning our mouth. In response, it sends a jolt of pain to the mouth, as if something was really burning.

Did you know that there is a scale to measure the intensity of 'heat' of some chilli peppers?

The Scoville scale, developed by American pharmacologist Wilbur Scoville in 1912, measures the level of capsaicin in a chilli. The higher the concentration of capsaicin, the hotter the chilli. The unit of measure for the Scoville scale is the Scoville Heat Unit (SHU).

Scoville Heat Unit (SHU)

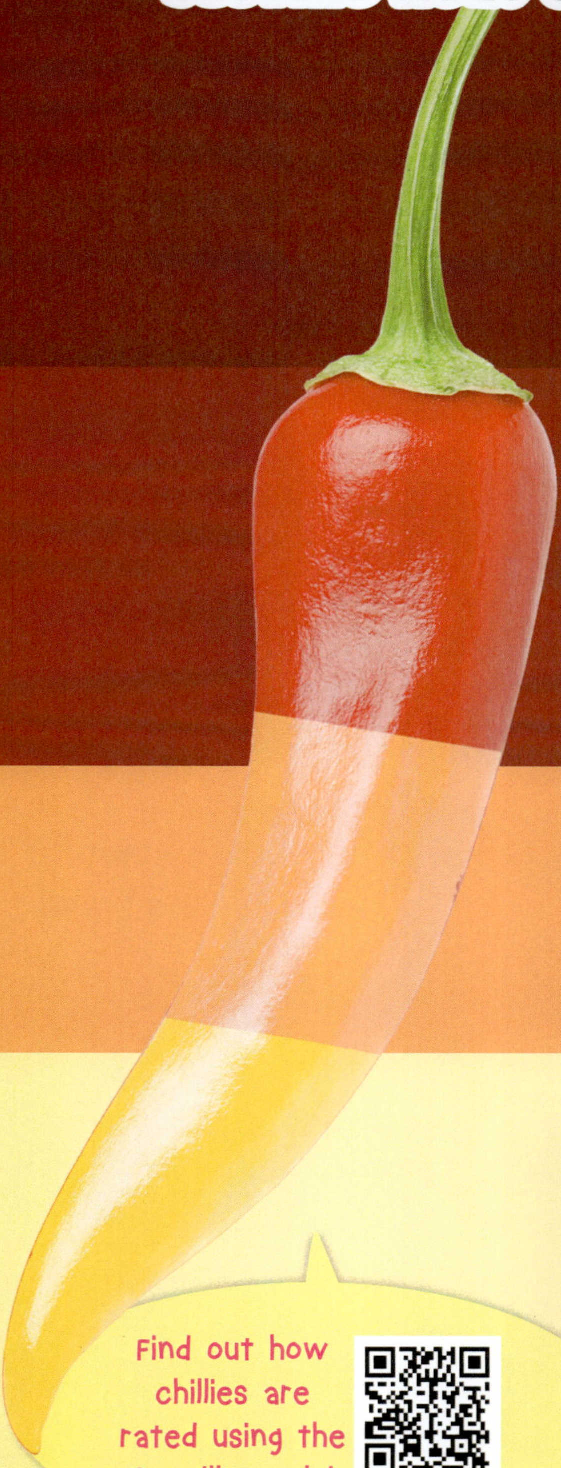

Carolina reaper

1.5–2.2 million SHUs

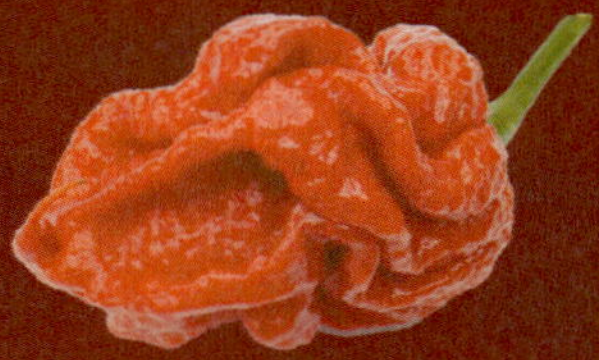

Red chilli padi
(bird's eye chilli)

**100,000–
225,000 SHUs**

Jalapeno

2,500–8,000 SHUs

Bell pepper

0 SHUs

Find out how chillies are rated using the Scoville scale!

Popping Spheres

Are you a fan of bubble tea? Popping boba are a common feature in many types of bubble tea. Popping boba are small translucent spheres that consist of a thin membrane containing a flavoured liquid. The spheres burst in the mouth, releasing the liquid.

What's the science behind popping boba? Let's find out!

Popping boba are made using a method called spherification. In this method, the flavoured liquid is mixed with sodium alginate. Then, the resulting solution is gently dropped into a bath of calcium chloride. This creates perfect spheres enclosed by a thin membrane that pop in your mouth.

WORD WHIZ

membrane: a thin sheet or layer that encloses something

True or False?

Do you remember what you have learnt about food science so far? Test yourself with this quiz! Which sentences are true and which are false?

1. Our body needs vitamins and minerals in small amounts.
2. Fibre is a carbohydrate that gives us energy.
3. Butterflies visit flowers to feed on the petals.
4. Dry ice is the solid form of oxygen.
5. Dry ice changes directly from a solid to a gas.
6. Eating raw eggs can cause food poisoning.
7. Mushrooms are a type of plant.
8. Pasteurisation makes milk and juices last longer.
9. A fungus helps bread dough to rise.
10. Red chilli padi is the hottest chilli in the world.

Find the answers on page 55!

Project Work

The Recommended Daily Allowance (RDA) refers to the recommended daily levels of nutrients we need to take in to stay healthy. The RDA of a nutrient depends on factors such as age and gender. Let's find out if you are meeting the RDA for a nutrient such as calcium!

What you need

- A notebook
- The Internet
- A pen
- An adult to supervise

What you need to do

1. With the help of an adult, use a reliable website on the Internet to find your RDA for calcium.

2. Maintain a daily food diary. Write down everything you eat and find out how much calcium you took in. Record your meals for one week.

What I ate/drank	How much calcium it has
Breakfast • 1 cup of milk • 1 banana	 • 300 mg • 6 mg
Lunch	
Dinner	

3. At the end of the week, check your food diary to see if you are meeting your RDA for calcium. If not, find out what are some good sources of calcium and include them in your diet.

Answers

Mix and Match (page 17)

Potato – stem

Spinach – leaf

Tomato – fruit

Pea – seed

Carrot – root

Detective Work (page 44)

(a) Sushi

(b) Taco

(c) Dosa/Thosai

(d) Kimchi

(e) Pizza

(f) Thai green curry

(g) Lasagna

(h) Laksa

True or False? (page 52)

1. True
2. False
3. False
4. False
5. True
6. True
7. False
8. True
9. True
10. False

I'M A FUTURE SCIENTIST!

The *I'm a Future Scientist!* series of full-colour books for 6–12 year olds will spark sustained interest in scientific fields, such as botany, zoology, marine biology, conservation and the environment, astronomy, and many more, delivering primary-school-level Science learning points in an engaging and relatable way! Through clearly written educational articles, fun cartoons, suggested hands-on activities, as well as full-colour photographs and illustrations, these books are the perfect companions for budding scientists to delve further into a wide range of scientific fields.

Read them all!

WS Education

Email sales@wspc.com for sales enquiries and bulk purchase opportunities.